CRYPTID GUIDES: CREATURES OF FOLKLORE

GUIDE TO BIGFOOT

A Crabtree Branches Book

BY CARRIE GLEASON

Crabtree Publishing
crabtreebooks.com

Developed and produced by Plan B Book Packagers
www.planbbookpackagers.com
Art director: Rosie Gowsell Pattison

Crabtree editor: Ellen Rodger
Prepress technician: Margaret Salter
Production coordinator: Katherine Berti
Proofreader: Melissa Boyce

Photographs:
Pg 8 Rosie Gowsell; all other images Shutterstock.com.

Crabtree Publishing

crabtreebooks.com   800-387-7650

Hardcover	978-1-0396-6342-8
Paperback	978-1-0396-6391-6
Ebook (pdf)	978-1-0398-0717-4
Epub	978-1-0398-0744-0

Published in Canada
Crabtree Publishing
616 Welland Avenue
St. Catharines, Ontario
L2M 5V6

Published in the United States
Crabtree Publishing
347 Fifth Avenue
Suite 1402-145
New York, NY 10016

**Library and Archives Canada
Cataloguing in Publication**
Available at the Library and Archives Canada

**Library of Congress
Cataloging-in-Publication Data**
Available at the Library of Congress

Printed in the U.S.A./012023/CG20220815

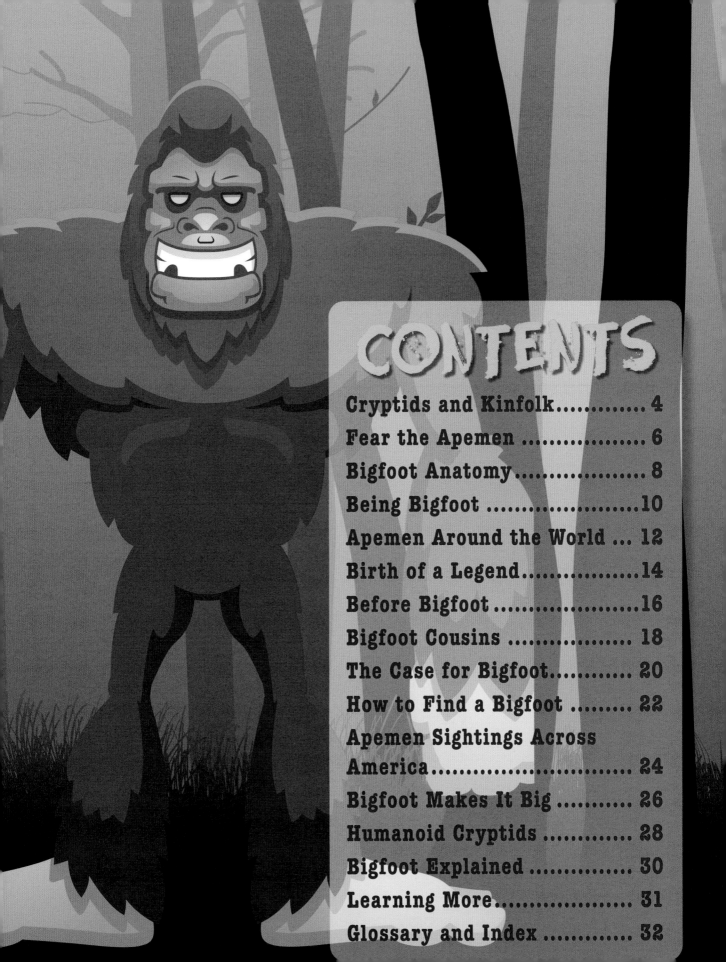

CONTENTS

CRYPTIDS and KINFOLK

This chart shows some of the best-known cryptids and creatures from folklore. How many of them do you think are real?

LAND DWELLER

UNDEAD

LIVING

SPIRIT

LIVING CORPSE

HUMANOID

Ghost

Zombie

Mummy

Werewolf

Werecat

Banshee

Grim Reaper

Ghoul

Vampire

Bigfoot

Mothman

Yeti

Yeren

Yowie

WHAT IS A BIGFOOT?

A bigfoot is a cryptid—a creature from folklore whose existence is not yet proven to be true. Cryptozoologists are people who search for and study these creatures. They gather stories from folklore and investigate reported sightings of cryptids. This book shows what is true, what is thought to be true, and what are outright lies and hoaxes about bigfoot. Could bigfoot be real? This Cryptid Guide will help you decide!

ANIMAL & HYBRID

Unicorn

Jackalope

Chupacabra

OTHERWORLDLY

GIANT

Ogre

Troll

Fairy

Elf

Nymph

SEA MONSTER

EXTRATERRESTRIAL

Alien

SWAMP MONSTER

Mermaid

Sea Serpent

LAKE MONSTER

Louisiana Swamp Monster

Leviathan

Loch Ness Monster

Ogopogo

Champ

FEAR THE APEMEN...

Imagine this: It's long ago, and you're walking in a forest. Tall trees are all around, and the ground is mossy and littered with fallen leaves and branches. You've moved to this neck of the woods because your father has a job building a road through the forest. It's too bad that the forest will soon be disturbed by cars and people, you think. Looking up, you see some branches high above your head that have been twisted in unusual ways. Strange, when there hasn't been a storm lately. Not watching where you're going, you almost fall into a large hole in the ground. Except this is no ordinary hole! It's shaped like a giant human foot, several times larger than yours. You hear a knocking sound coming from behind a tree and freeze. Who— or what—is there? You don't wait to find out! You turn and run as fast as you can. As you do, small rocks start whizzing past your head. Whatever it is in the forest, it doesn't want you there!

BIGFOOT BASICS

Bigfoot belong to a group of cryptids called apemen—creatures that are both ape-like and human-like. According to legends, bigfoot and other apemen live in thick forests or mountain regions, far away from people. The legend of bigfoot as we know it today began in 1958 in Humboldt County, California. But Indigenous peoples' **stories of wild, often hairy,** humanoid **creatures that live in forests** were around long before bigfoot. Bigfoot are one of the most hunted cryptids in the world, and although they prefer to keep to themselves, they often play a starring role in books, TV, and movies.

Bigfoot's name was made up by a Califormia newspaper reporter in 1958. This was after loggers discovered large, human-looking footprints and other strange, unexplained happenings at their camp.

OTHER HAIRY BEASTS

Werewolves

Werewolves come from European folklore. They are living people that transform into wolf form during a full moon. Werewolves have been said to attack and kill animals and humans.

Chupacabras

Chupacabras are cryptids first sighted in Puerto Rico in the 1990s. They are often described as dog-like. They drink the blood of livestock, such as sheep and goats.

Werecats

Werecats are creatures that are half human and half big cat (like a lion, tiger, or leopard). Werecat legends come from places where these big cats are top predators, such as Africa, Asia, and South America.

BIGFOOT ANATOMY

Bigfoot—they're giant, hairy, and muscular, known for their foul smell and large, human-like footprints. Here's how to spot a bigfoot.

Short neck

Long arms

Head shaped like an ape's

Human-like face with a flat nose and visible lips

Human-like eyes that may glow at night

Wide shoulders

Covered in black or brown shaggy hair

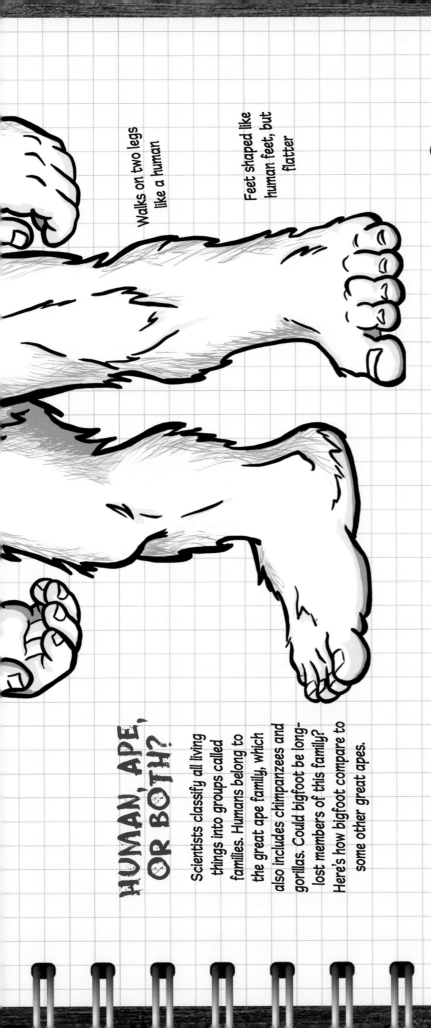

HUMAN, APE, OR BOTH?

Scientists classify all living things into groups called families. Humans belong to the great ape family, which also includes chimpanzees and gorillas. Could bigfoot be long-lost members of this family? Here's how bigfoot compare to some other great apes.

Walks on two legs like a human

Feet shaped like human feet, but flatter

CHIMPANZEE
Height: 5 feet (1.5 m)
Weight: 130 pounds (59 kg)
Lifespan: 30 years

HUMAN
Height: 5 feet 7 inches (1.7 m)
Weight: 150 pounds (68 kg)
Lifespan: 72 years

GORILLA
Height: 6 feet (1.8 m)
Weight: 440 pounds (200 kg)
Lifespan: 40 years

BIGFOOT
Height: 10 feet (3 m)
Weight: 600 pounds (272 kg)
Lifespan: Unknown

BEING BIGFOOT

Bigfoot are masters of their territory, which stretches for hundreds of miles in forested areas of North America. Have you ever been in a forest and felt like you were being watched? Chances are that a bigfoot will know when you are in its territory, but you will never see it...unless it wants to be seen.

A BIGFOOT MIGHT BE NEARBY IF...

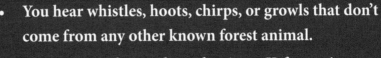
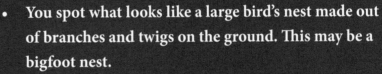

- You find human-like footprints that are up to 20 inches (50 cm) long.

- The air smells like rotten eggs. You can smell a bigfoot long before you see it, and long after it's gone.

- You hear the sound of wood knocking against wood. This is one way they communicate.

- You hear whistles, hoots, chirps, or growls that don't come from any other known forest animal.

- You see upright tree branches in an X-formation or a tipi-like structure. This could be a bigfoot marking its territory.

- You see tree branches about 8 to 10 feet (2.4 to 3 m) off the ground that have been snapped in half or twisted.

- You find an animal carcass in a tree. Bigfoot researchers debate whether a bigfoot kills and eats animals or whether it eats mostly berries, bark, nuts, and plants.

- You spot what looks like a large bird's nest made out of branches and twigs on the ground. This may be a bigfoot nest.

- You have a feeling like you are being watched. A bigfoot can remain very still for long periods of time and if you look very closely, you may be able to spot one watching you from between tree branches or behind rocks.

It is not known how many bigfoot there are, or whether they live alone or in groups. Some bigfoot researchers say that each bigfoot has its own territory, while others say that there are groups living together in one territory. There have been reported sightings of single bigfoot and of males and females together. A lumberjack even claimed that he was kidnapped by a bigfoot family made up of a male, a female, and two bigfoot children in British Columbia, Canada, in 1924.

TIP: Watch out for rocks being thrown at you. This is a bigfoot's way of saying, "Go away!"

APEMEN AROUND THE WORLD

THE WIDE WORLD OF APEMEN

Bigfoot may be the most famous of the apemen, but others are said to live all over the world. These apemen also prefer to stay hidden, living in areas with terrain that is too difficult for humans to easily visit. They are described as looking similar to bigfoot. This map shows some of the bigfoot-like cryptids found around the world.

1 In Canada, a bigfoot is usually called a sasquatch, and is believed to be the same creature as the American bigfoot. It mostly lives in the forests of British Columbia and Alberta.

2 Most bigfoot sightings in the U.S. are in the Pacific Northwest. But there have been bigfoot sightings across the country, and sightings of other types of apemen too.

1 Canada

2 United States

3 South America

4 Central Asia

5 Africa

6 China

7 Japan

8 Indonesia

9 India

10 Australia

5 The agogwe comes from legends of East Africa, where it lives in forests. It is reported to be smaller than a bigfoot, at just 2 to 5 feet (0.6 to 1.5 m) tall, and has copper-colored hair.

8 The orang pendek lives in the mountainous forest of the Indonesian island of Sumatra. It is said to be just 2.5 to 5 feet (0.8 to 1.5 m) tall.

10 The yowie lives in the Australian outback, a large dry region in the middle of the country. It has a wide, flat nose.

4 The almas lives in central Asia in three mountain ranges, the Caucasus, Pamir, and Altai. It has reddish-brown hair all over its body and is said to make tools and clothes.

7 The hibagon of Japan is said to be about 5 feet (1.5 m) tall, with reddish-brown hair with white patches. It smells like rotting flesh.

9 The mande barung is reported to live in the forests of northeast India. This shy apeman has black hair, and eats bananas and tree bark.

3 The mapinguari lives in the Amazon rain forest. It has been described as either an ape-like creature or a giant ground sloth. Some reports say it has only one eye in the middle of its forehead and a mouth in its stomach.

6 The yeren from Chinese folklore lives in forested mountains. It is said to raid villages for food and to laugh when it sees a human.

BEWARE: A FACT!

Although some other members of the great ape family can stand or even walk on two legs for short distances, humans are the only ones that always walk on two legs. This is because of differences in human skeletons versus those of apes. The ability to walk on two legs is called bipedalism.

BIRTH OF A LEGEND

There have been thousands of reported sightings and encounters with bigfoot. But these aren't considered real, hard evidence that bigfoot exist. So, what did people do? They faked evidence! Here are some of the most famous stories of bigfoot encounters.

ARE THEY HOAXES OR THE REAL DEAL?

BATTLE (OR BULLIES?) AT APE CANYON

Ape Canyon in Washington got its name from a supposed bigfoot encounter there in 1924. As the story goes, five gold miners were camped out in a cabin in the canyon. Two of them went to get water from a nearby spring, where they saw a 7-foot-tall (2 m) ape-like creature covered in black hair. They shot at it, and it ran away. That night, the creature returned with others and attacked their cabin. The creatures shook the cabin, threw stones at it, and tried to break in. By daylight, the creatures had left. The story ran in the local papers and an investigation took place to try and find the creatures, but none were located.

 VERDICT?

UNKNOWN: Fifty years after the "Battle at Ape Canyon," a logger came forward claiming that he and his uncle had attacked the cabin to play a joke on the miners. Other people say that the incident may have been a joke played on the miners by young people from a nearby camp.

"WHAT IS IT?"

One of the earliest newspaper reports of a bigfoot was in the *Daily Colonist* in Victoria, British Columbia, in 1884. The front-page story was titled "What is it?" and said that a half-boy, half-gorilla creature had been found by railway workers in Yale. The men who found the creature named it "Jacko." Another local paper wrote that the creature had been taken to jail, where 200 people had come to see it.

 VERDICT?

HOAX: A few days later, it was exposed that the story had been a hoax when none of the supposed visitors who went to see the creature in jail could be found.

BLUFFING AT BLUFF CREEK?

In 1958, a story ran in the *Humboldt Times* about workers in a forest who noticed large footprints and strange happenings at their camp in Bluff Creek, California. A heavy drum of gasoline was missing, and a 700-pound (318 kg) tire had been rolled into a ditch. Plaster casts were made of the footprints, but no one had actually seen the creature that made them. The newspaper called it "Big Foot," and the story was picked up by other newspapers across the country.

VERDICT?

UNKNOWN: This story made bigfoot famous. For many years it was believed to be true. Then, in 2002, one of the owners of the company died and his family came forward saying they had found a set of carved wooden feet that had been used to make the footprints. Whether or not the story was a hoax is still hotly debated by bigfoot researchers today.

CAUGHT ON VIDEO?

In 1967, the first video recording of a bigfoot was taken by two men in northern California who were shooting a movie about…finding bigfoot! The bigfoot's appearance in the film is less than 60 seconds long. It shows a tall, human-like form covered in black hair and walking on two legs.

VERDICT?

UNKNOWN: For years, people debated whether the creature in the video, known as the Patterson-Gimlin film, was really a bigfoot or a person dressed in a gorilla suit. In recent years, people claiming to have been involved in the hoax have come forward, including the man who created the gorilla suit and the man who wore it. The two men who made the video always claimed it was real.

WAS A BIGFOOT FINALLY CAPTURED?

In 2008, a well-known bigfoot hunter claimed that he had killed a bigfoot in Georgia and that he had the body to prove it. The body was packed in ice and examined by a bigfoot researcher who said that he had measured it and saw that it had real body parts inside. A press conference was held and stories about it appeared in the news.

VERDICT?

HOAX: When the body thawed, it was discovered that it was a gorilla costume stuffed with body parts from dead animals. The bigfoot hunter admitted that it had been a hoax, and then he tried it again a few years later with another body! The hunter still claims that he has a real bigfoot body hidden away.

BEFORE BIGFOOT

Legends of ape-like creatures that live in the forests of North America were around long before bigfoot and European settlers. Indigenous peoples across the continent told different stories of "wild men" or "hairy men" who were supernatural beings. Here are some of them.

SASQUATCH

A bigfoot's other name, sasquatch, comes from the Salish word *sásq'ets*, meaning "wild man." For the Salish-speaking Indigenous peoples of the Pacific coast, Sásq'ets is a powerful supernatural creature in the shape of a very large and hairy wild man.

BAKWAS

The Kwakwaka'wakw people of British Columbia tell stories of a creature called Bakwas, or "the wild man of the woods." Bakwas is covered in green hair and offers lost travelers food. If the travelers accept the food, they will turn into ghosts.

GLUE-KEEK

Legends from the Quinault people of coastal Washington tell of a bigfoot-like creature called Glue-keek that has glowing eyes, legs as large as tree trunks, and big feet.

BOQS

Boqs are large, hairy men of the forests from legends of the Chinookan-language speakers of the Pacific Northwest coast. Sometimes boqs are dangerous monsters, but other times they are shy and timid. Boqs are also called skookum, which has become another name for bigfoot.

ROCK PAINTING

At the foothills of the Sierra Nevada mountain range in California is a sacred site for the Yokut people. There, rock paintings believed to be between 500 and 1,000 years old show a creation story that includes a bigfoot family. Creation stories are important to different cultures because they tell of how the world began and how a particular people came to be in it. The bigfoot-like creatures in the paintings have long, shaggy hair and are found alongside drawings of real animals such as coyotes, beavers, and birds, as well as humans.

FEARSOME CRITTERS

In the early days of logging in North America, workers spent long periods of time in the wilderness. To pass the time and to play jokes on one another, the loggers made up stories about imaginary creatures they called "fearsome critters." These critters had funny names such as the snallygaster, the gillygaloo bird, and the gumerboo. Some of these fearsome critters have lived on to become cryptids today, such as the jackalope, a hare with the antlers of an antelope.

BIGFOOT COUSINS

Relatives of bigfoot make their homes from the highest mountain range in the world, the Himalayas, to the dry Australian outback. Here's how bigfoot's three most famous cousins compare.

Yeti

Aka:
The Abominable Snowman

Habitat:
The snow-covered Himalayan mountain ranges between India, Nepal, and Tibet

Appearance:
May be slightly smaller than a bigfoot. Covered in brown, gray, or white hair. May have large, sharp teeth.

Behavior:
Some reports say that the yeti is gentle and helpful, while others say that it is strong enough to throw boulders. The yeti has been said to howl, whistle, and roar like a lion.

APES FROM LONG AGO

One theory about apemen like bigfoot and their cousins is that they may be descendants of prehistoric apes. *Gigantopithecus blacki* is a prehistoric ape that lived 2.6 million to 11,700 years ago in what is now southern China. The only fossil remains that have been discovered are teeth and jaws. From these, scientists think that the apes may have been 10 feet (3 m) tall, weighed 1,100 pounds (500 kg), and ate mainly bamboo and fruit. *Gigantopithecus blacki* are believed to be the largest apes that ever lived.

Yowie
Aka: Yahoo

Habitat: The Australian outback

Appearance:
Stands 7 to 11 feet (2 to 34 m) tall,
covered in brown or light-brown hair.
Has a wide nose.

Behavior:
The yowie is generally believed to be timid
or shy, but may turn aggressive. It is said
to move super fast.

Yeren
Aka: Wild Man

Habitat:
Forested mountains of
central China. Lives in caves.

Appearance:
Reported to be between 6
and 8 feet (1.8 to 24 m) tall,
with a slimmer body than a
bigfoot. It has orange-brown
or red-black hair.

Behavior:
The yeren is believed to be
more aggressive than other
apemen. It raids villages for
food and kidnaps female
villagers. It is said to be
strong and speedy.

THE CASE FOR BIGFOOT

The quest to prove whether or not bigfoot are real has been taken seriously. Bigfoot researchers have formed organizations to investigate sightings and find evidence of bigfoot. Scientists, governments, and different types of experts have all helped out. This timeline shows some of the real-life attempts to find and protect bigfoot.

Date: 1969

The first law to protect bigfoot is passed in Skamania County, Washington. The penalty for killing a bigfoot is a fine and time in jail.

Date: 1976

The U.S. Federal Bureau of Investigation (FBI), gets involved. They agree to analyze 15 hairs thought to be from a bigfoot. Forty years later, they make the bigfoot file public, which says that the hairs belong to a deer.

Date: 1972–'75

The Berry Morehead tapes capture 90 minutes of what is claimed to be bigfoot sounds. The sounds include whoops, screams, human-sounding voices, and knocking sounds. Many years later, a retired cryptologic linguist from the U.S. Navy studies the tapes and determines that the sounds are a non-human language and are not fake.

Date: 2000

A plaster cast of a print that some believe may belong to a bigfoot is taken in Washington. Called the Skookum Cast, it is examined by an anthropologist at Idaho State University who studies primate footprints. He says that the cast may be an imprint of a sitting bigfoot.

Date: 2013

A bigfoot researcher gives bigfoot the scientific name *Homo sapiens cognatus*. The name is approved by ZooBank, an internationally recognized organization that keeps official lists of scientific names.

Date: 1995

The Bigfoot Field Researchers Organization is founded. It is the first and largest organization of people dedicated to investigating bigfoot.

Date: 2012

In England, Oxford University researchers put out a call for hair samples from apemen around the world to be sent to them for DNA testing. In a report released two years later, they find that none of the hairs tested came from a bigfoot-type creature, but they also say that their findings are not proof that bigfoot aren't real.

Date: 2018

A Canadian bigfoot tracker goes to court in the province of British Columbia to make the case that bigfoot are real. It is the first time that the case for bigfoot's existence is heard in court. The claim is dismissed due to lack of evidence.

HOW TO FIND A BIGFOOT

Bigfoot have been sighted all across North America. If you enjoy camping and exploring the outdoors, bigfoot tracking might be for you. Here's what you need to know before you set out to track a bigfoot.

GETTING STARTED

You will need:

- camping or outdoor gear, such as appropriate clothing and shoes, water, food, and bug repellent
- a local wildlife book and possibly a map
- a tape measure
- a journal, camera, video recorder, or smartphone

TIP: It is not safe to look for a bigfoot alone. Bring a friend or family member. If you do see a bigfoot, it will help to have other witnesses to back up your claim.

Before you go:

- read reports of past sightings to find out about places where bigfoot may be
- research wildlife in the area where you are looking so you don't confuse other animal tracks for bigfoot tracks

WHERE TO LOOK

Look for bigfoot in places that:

- have fresh water, such as a nearby river or stream
- have a food supply, such as berries and nuts
- have trees and caves that bigfoot may use for shelter

FINDING A BIGFOOT

- Listen for bigfoot sounds. These may include whistles, hollers, hoots, and wood-knocking sounds.
- Pay attention to what you smell. Bigfoot have a strong odor.
- Look for bigfoot evidence. This may include hairs, animal droppings, broken branches, and nests.

TIP:

If you see a bigfoot or any other wildlife, do not approach it! Bigfoot do not want to be bothered.

IF YOU FIND A BIGFOOT FOOTPRINT

- Use your tape measure to measure both the length and width.
- Take photographs or make sketches of it in your journal.
- Make a plaster cast of the impression.

HOW TO MAKE A FOOTPRINT CAST

YOU WILL NEED:

 water

 plaster of Paris (available at craft stores)

 a small container for mixing your plaster

 a spoon or spatula

INSTRUCTIONS:

1. Mix the plaster and water in your container until it looks like whipped cream.

2. Use the spoon or spatula to fill the footprint with plaster.

3. When the plaster is hard and dry, peel it out of the ground. Flip it over. Ta-da! You now have a cast of the footprint.

THE CRYPTID RECORD

Cryptozoology's #1 Source for Sightings

Apemen Sightings Across America

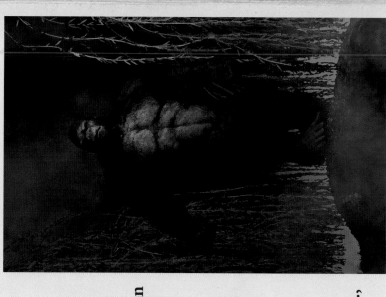

Reported Sightings

Across the country, people have claimed to have spotted other types of apemen, and cryptozoologists believe that these are separate creatures from bigfoot. Reports of sightings are important for cryptozoologists. They interview people who have encountered cryptids and read about past sightings to try to put together the full story of a cryptid. These are some examples of real-life sightings.

Skunk Ape
Florida

In 1974, a man reported to police that he had hit a Florida skunk ape with his car. Police looked for the creature but couldn't find it. The man described the creature as between 5 to 7 feet (1.5 to 2 m) tall, with reddish-brown hair, and smelling like a skunk. Later reports have said that it walks on two legs, has four toes on each foot, and can climb trees, where it also sleeps. Most sightings have been in the forests and swamps of the southeastern U.S., especially the Florida Everglades.

Honey Island Swamp Monster
Louisiana

The Honey Island Swamp Monster was first sighted in 1963 by a retired air traffic controller. He described the creature as having gray hair, wide shoulders, and a human-looking face with red or yellow eyes. The man made casts of its footprints, showing that it only had four toes on each foot. After the man's death, his granddaughter also found he had taken a video of the monster. Many sightings have since been reported.

Boggy Creek Monster
Arkansas

The Boggy Creek Monster is also known as the Fouke Monster. It is thought to be very vicious and dangerous. In 1971, it was reported to have attacked a family at their home, damaging the porch, a window, and the siding of the house before being chased off. Tracks showed that it had three toes on each foot. It has been described as 7 feet (2 m) tall, weighing 300 pounds (136 kg), and swinging its long arms like a monkey when it runs. A local radio station offered a $1,000 reward for its capture, but the creature was never caught.

Momo the Monster
Missouri

In the summer of 1972, terror struck Louisiana, Missouri. A family saw a 7-foot-tall (2 m) creature covered in dark hair. It had a pumpkin-shaped head and was carrying a dead dog. A 20-person search party was organized to hunt down the creature, but it was not found. Momo, as the monster was called, has not been reported since. What happened to it is a mystery.

BIGFOOT MAKES IT BIG

What do you picture when you think of bigfoot today? Are they still wild, fearsome creatures, or kind, gentle protectors of forests and wildlife? This timeline looks at how the image of bigfoot in popular culture has changed over time.

2002
The first Sasquatch! Music Festival is held in George, Washington. Festival-goers camp outdoors during the two-day concert every Memorial Day weekend until it is canceled in 2018.

1993
Squatch the Sasquatch becomes the team mascot for the National Basketball Association (NBA) team the Seattle SuperSonics.

2010
Quatchi, a young sasquatch that wears blue earmuffs and dreams of being a hockey goalie, is created as one of the mascots for the Winter Olympics in Vancouver, British Columbia.

2013
The horror film *Willow Creek* is released. It is about two people who go to Humboldt County to make a bigfoot documentary, but they go missing. The bigfoot in the movie is never shown.

2020
During the COVID-19 pandemic, a bigfoot is used in public service announcements to encourage people to maintain physical distancing.

2020
In *Bigfoot Family*, a children's animated movie, a bigfoot decides to use his fame to help protect wildlife against an oil company. He is helped by his son, who has a human mother.

START
HERE

1961
The town of Willow Creek, in Humboldt County, California, hosts its first Bigfoot Days/Daze festival, which celebrates the bigfoot legend, and the logging history of the area. The festival still runs today.

1964
The character of Bumble, an abominable snowman, appears in the Christmas movie *Rudolph the Red-Nosed Reindeer*. Bumble suffers from a toothache in the movie, which makes him cranky.

1970
The American sci-fi film *Bigfoot* is released. It shows Bigfoot as a fearsome movie monster, like King Kong or Godzilla.

1987
The family adventure movie *Harry and the Hendersons* is released. In the movie, Harry is a friendly bigfoot who bonds with a family that tries to keep him safe from a bigfoot hunter.

1975
The first "Bigfoot" monster truck is created by off-roader Bob Chandler. The truck was shown at tractor pulls and car shows and immediately became popular because of its big tires.

2013
Sasquatched! The Musical hits the stage. It follows the story of a bigfoot named Arthur and a boy named Sam who encounter a TV crew searching for bigfoot, a pair of bigfoot hoaxers, and park rangers.

2015
The U.S. Forest Service issues a news release claiming that bigfoot are real. The news release is an April Fool's Day joke, meant to raise awareness about forest protection.

2018
In the animated movie *Smallfoot*, a yeti finds a human, or "smallfoot," but his yeti family doesn't believe him. They think that humans are cryptids!

2019
The Oregon State Fire Marshal's Office launches a campaign to prevent forest fires using a bigfoot as the spokesperson.

2019
Missing Link, an animated movie about a cryptozoologist who tracks down a lonely bigfoot, is released. The cryptozoologist helps the bigfoot find his long-lost yeti cousins in the Himalayas.
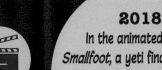

HUMANOID CRYPTIDS

A bigfoot is what's referred to as a humanoid cryptid—a creature that is any mix of human and animal. Humanoid cryptids may have some or all of these characteristics:

- the ability to walk on two legs like a human
- hands, or paws, that are more similar to a human's than an animal's
- human-like facial features, in particular the eyes, as well as a human-sounding voice
- near-human intelligence

Here are some examples of other types of humanoid cryptids from foklore.

MOTHMEN

Mothmen are half human and half winged animal. They have been reported to be 7 to 10 feet (2 to 3 m) tall, with large wings and glowing red eyes. Mothmen sightings occur near graveyards, abandoned factories, or mines. Some people think they may be a warning of danger.

DOGMEN

Closely related to werewolves, dogmen are any mix of human and canine creature. There have been many reported sightings of dogmen in North America.

GOATMEN

Goatmen are tall creatures that are half human and half goat. Most sightings have been reported in Louisiana, Maryland, and Texas. In ancient Roman mythology, a satyr was a woodland god that looked like a man but had a goat's ears, tail, legs, and horns.

DEER PEOPLE

Sightings of deer people have mostly occurred in the United States. They are reported to either have horns and the face of a deer with the body of a human, or a human face and the legs and hooves of a deer.

GATORMEN

Gatormen are half alligator and half human. They belong to a group of cryptids called lizardmen. Gatormen are covered in scales and walk on two legs like a human. They make their homes in algae-covered swamps.

Bigfoot Explained

Hair samples believed to belong to bigfoot have often turned out after testing to belong to deer, bears, humans, or other known animals. Some people believe that most bigfoot sightings are actually bears standing on their hind legs. Bears usually walk on all fours, but may stand on their back legs if they have an injured front paw.

Seeing Faces

Look at the photo of a piece of wood below. Do you see a human face? It is possible that people who have reported seeing a bigfoot's human-like face aren't really seeing a human face at all, it is just their mind playing tricks on them. Pareidolia is the word used to describe wanting to see something familiar in an object.

From Cryptid to Species

Until bones, DNA, or a live bigfoot is captured and studied by science, bigfoot will remain cryptids. It could happen one day, as it did for these animals once thought to be cryptids.

Platypus, cryptid until 1799

Okapi, aka the African unicorn, cryptid until 1901

Gorilla, cryptid until 1902

Komodo dragon, cryptid until 1910

Giant squid, cryptid until 2004

LEARNING MORE

Want to know more about cryptids, myths, and monsters such as the ones described in this book? Here are some resources to check out on your cryptid-hunting quest.

Books

Behind the Legend: Bigfoot by Erin Peabody. Little Bee Books, 2017.

Monster Science: Could Monsters Survive (and Thrive!) in the Real World? by Helaine Becker. Kids Can Press, 2016.

Tales of the Cryptids by Kelly Milner Halls, Rick C. Spears, and Roxyanne Young. Millbrook Press, 2006.

TV and Films

Monstrum is a series of videos created by PBS about monsters, myths, and legends.

Find the videos on the PBS website at:

www.pbs.org/show/monstrum/

Websites

The Centre for Fortean Zoology is a cryptozoology organization that researches cryptids from around the world. They produce a weekly TV show, books, and magazines about cryptids.

www.cfz.org.uk/

GLOSSARY

anthropologist Someone who studies human beings and their cultures, from prehistoric times to today

carcass The body of a dead animal

cryptologic linguist A person who identifies and analyzes foreign communication

descendant Related to something that existed at an earlier time

dismissed No longer being considered in court

DNA Molecules, or small particles, in cells that contain genetic code

folklore The stories, customs, and beliefs that people of a certain place share and pass down through the generations

hoax An act or object passed off as real and meant to fool someone

humanoid Something that is not human, but has the appearance or behavior of one

Indigenous peoples The first people to live in a place

plaster cast An object made by filling a mold or hollow shape with a material called plaster, which hardens when it dries

popular culture The movies, music, TV, books, and fashion that everyone is interested in at a certain time

predator An animal that hunts another animal

prehistoric A time before recorded history

primate A member of the group of mammals that includes apes, monkeys, and humans

scientific name The formal name of an animal that is used by scientists

settler A person who moves to a new place. Also called a colonist.

supernatural A force that is beyond normal understanding

terrain The physical features of an area of land

INDEX